W9-AAS-506

Table of Contents

p.8

p.27

p.41

p.45

Classic Deviled Eggs

MAKES 12 HALVES

PREP TIME: 30 MINUTES

- 6 **hard-cooked eggs, halved**
- ¼ **cup Hellmann's® or Best Foods® Real Mayonnaise**
- 1 **teaspoon Hellmann's® or Best Foods® Dijonnaise™ Creamy Dijon Mustard**
- ½ **teaspoon white vinegar**
- ¼ **teaspoon salt**

1. Remove egg yolks, reserving egg whites.

2. Mash egg yolks in small bowl. Stir in remaining ingredients. Spoon or pipe into egg whites. Chill, if desired. Garnish, if desired, with parsley and sprinkle with paprika.

Variation: For a different taste…add 1 tablespoon pickle relish or finely chopped sweet pickles; OR 2 tablespoons cooked crumbled bacon; OR 1 tablespoon chopped green onion, ¾ teaspoon chili powder and hot pepper sauce to taste.

Substitution: Also terrific with Hellmann's® or Best Foods® Light Mayonnaise or Hellmann's® or Best Foods® Canola Cholesterol Free Mayonnaise.

Note: Make a double recipe because this party classic disappears fast!

Tip: To easily fill eggs, spoon filling into small resealable plastic bag and cut a small hole in one corner. Pipe into egg whites.

Creamy Mango Salsa

MAKES 4 SERVINGS

PREP TIME: 10 MINUTES

- ¼ cup Hellmann's® or Best Foods® Light Mayonnaise
- 1 tablespoon lime juice
- ½ teaspoon ground cumin
- 2 cups quartered grape tomatoes or cherry tomatoes
- 1 medium ripe mango, peeled and chopped
- ½ cup chopped red onion
- 1 medium jalapeño pepper, finely chopped (optional)
- 1 teaspoon chopped fresh cilantro (optional)
- Corn chips (optional)

Blend Hellmann's® or Best Foods® Light Mayonnaise with lime juice and cumin in medium bowl. Stir in remaining ingredients. Serve with chips.

Tip: Use Hellmann's® or Best Foods® Mayonnaise any time you need a flavor boost. For example, just add a little to the yolk mixture to kick up the taste of deviled eggs.

Snacks and Starters — 5

Hellmann's® Easiest-Ever Dipping Sauces

MAKES ½ TO ¾ CUP DIP

PREP TIME: 5 MINUTES

By simply adding just two ingredients to Hellmann's® Mayonnaise you can make these delicious dips!

½ cup Hellmann's® or Best Foods® Real or Light Mayonnaise

Stir the following ingredients into ½ cup Hellmann's® or Best Foods® Real or Light Mayonnaise:

For an **ITALIAN DIPPING SAUCE,** stir in 1 jar (7 ounces) roasted red peppers, drained and finely chopped, and ½ teaspoon red wine vinegar. Great for spreading on assorted crackers, thinly sliced Italian bread or fresh vegetable crudités.

For a **BLUE CHEESE DIPPING SAUCE,** stir in ¼ cup crumbled blue cheese and 2 tablespoons milk. Great with spicy chicken wings or barbecued chicken or beef.

For a **WASABI DIPPING SAUCE,** stir in 3 tablespoons prepared wasabi and 1 tablespoon milk. Great for dipping shrimp cocktail or spreading on roast beef or deli sandwiches for an extra kick!

For a **CREAMY PARMESAN DIPPING SAUCE,** stir in ¼ cup grated Parmesan cheese and 2 tablespoons milk. Great with fresh celery sticks, bell pepper strips or bread sticks.

For a **BUFFALO DIPPING SAUCE,** stir in 1 tablespoon cayenne pepper sauce and 1 tablespoon milk. Adds great flavor to vegetable crudités.

Honey Mustard Chicken Fingers

MAKES 5 SERVINGS

PREP TIME: 15 MINUTES
COOK TIME: 10 MINUTES

These pick-up-and-go crispy chicken fingers
are sure to please the pickiest of eaters.

- 6 tablespoons Hellmann's® or Best Foods® Light Mayonnaise
- 1 tablespoon honey mustard
- 1 pound boneless, skinless chicken breasts, cut into strips
- 1½ cups finely crushed cornflakes
- ¼ cup grated Parmesan cheese

1. Preheat oven to 425°F. Combine Hellmann's® or Best Foods® Light Mayonnaise with honey mustard in medium bowl; reserve ½ for dipping.

2. Add chicken to remaining Mayonnaise mixture; stir to coat. Mix cornflakes with Parmesan cheese, then roll chicken in crumbs.

3. Arrange on ungreased baking sheet. Bake 10 minutes or until chicken is thoroughly cooked. Serve with reserved honey mustard sauce.

Hellmann's® Creamy Spinach Dip

MAKES 4 CUPS DIP

PREP TIME: 5 MINUTES
CHILL TIME: 2 HOURS

Whether served in an impressive bread bowl or a simple ceramic bowl, this dip is always a hit.

- 1 container (16 ounces) sour cream
- 1 package (10 ounces) frozen chopped spinach, cooked, cooled and squeezed dry
- 1 cup Hellmann's® or Best Foods® Real Mayonnaise
- 1 package Knorr® Vegetable recipe mix

Combine all ingredients in medium bowl. Chill 2 hours.

Substitutions: Try using 1 container (16 ounces) nonfat plain Greek yogurt instead of sour cream.

Also terrific with Hellmann's® or Best Foods® Canola Cholesterol Free Mayonnaise or Hellmann's® or Best Foods® Light Mayonnaise.

Mini Reuben Skewers with Dipping Sauce

MAKES 40 SERVINGS

PREP TIME: 10 MINUTES

- ⅓ cup **Hellmann's® or Best Foods® Real Mayonnaise**
- ⅓ cup **Wish-Bone® Thousand Island Dressing**
- 1 can (8 ounces) **sauerkraut, drained and coarsely chopped**
- 4 **thin slices rye bread, crust removed**
- 8 ounces **sliced Swiss cheese**
- 8 ounces **sliced cooked corned beef or pastrami**

1. Combine Hellmann's® or Best Foods® Real Mayonnaise, Wish-Bone® Thousand Island Dressing and sauerkraut in medium bowl; set aside.

2. Top 2 bread slices evenly with cheese, corned beef, then remaining bread. Cut each sandwich into 20 cubes and secure with wooden toothpicks. Serve with dipping sauce.

Sweet Potato Fries with BBQ Mayonnaise

MAKES 8 SERVINGS

PREP TIME: 15 MINUTES
COOK TIME: 35 MINUTES

- 2 **pounds sweet potatoes or yams, peeled and cut into 2-inch-long thin wedges**
- 1 **cup Hellmann's® or Best Foods® Real Mayonnaise, divided**
- ¼ **cup barbecue sauce**

1. Preheat oven to 425°F. Line two rimmed baking sheets with aluminum foil, then spray with no-stick cooking spray; set aside.

2. Combine potatoes with ½ cup Hellmann's® or Best Foods® Real Mayonnaise in large bowl; toss to coat. Arrange potatoes on prepared pans.

3. Bake 20 minutes. Rotate pans and bake an additional 15 minutes or until potatoes are golden and crisp.

4. Meanwhile, combine remaining ½ cup Mayonnaise with barbecue sauce in small bowl. Serve with fries.

Creamy Salsa Potato Salad

MAKES 8 SERVINGS

PREP TIME: 15 MINUTES
COOK TIME: 10 MINUTES

- 2 **pounds new potatoes, cut into bite-size pieces**
- ¾ **cup Hellmann's® or Best Foods® Real Mayonnaise**
- ¾ **cup salsa**
- 1 **cup shredded Cheddar cheese (about 4 ounces)**
- ½ **cup sliced pitted ripe olives (optional)**
- 1 **green onion, thinly sliced**

1. Cover potatoes with water in 4-quart saucepot; bring to a boil over medium-high heat. Reduce heat to low and simmer uncovered 10 minutes or until potatoes are tender. Drain; DO NOT RINSE. Let cool slightly.

2. Toss potatoes with remaining ingredients. Serve chilled or at room temperature.

3. Garnish, if desired, with additional sliced green onions or chopped cilantro. Season, if desired, with cayenne pepper sauce.

Chicken Nugget Sliders

MAKES 4 SERVINGS

PREP TIME: 20 MINUTES

Fun little sandwiches that the kids can help make.

- ¼ cup Hellmann's® or Best Foods® Real Mayonnaise
- 2 tablespoons ketchup
- 12 party-size potato rolls, split
- 12 frozen or refrigerated chicken nuggets*, cooked according to package directions
- 3 slices Cheddar or muenster cheese, cut into quarters
- 3 slices bacon, crisp-cooked and broken into 12 pieces
- 12 small iceberg lettuce leaves

Try with your favorite homemade chicken nugget recipe or chicken tenders cut into pieces.

Combine Hellmann's® or Best Foods® Real Mayonnaise with ketchup in small bowl; spread on bottom of rolls. Top with remaining ingredients.

Creamy Artichoke Bruschetta

MAKES 10 SERVINGS

PREP TIME: 15 MINUTES
COOK TIME: 1 MINUTE

- 1 jar (6 ounces) marinated artichoke hearts, drained and chopped
- ¼ cup Hellmann's® or Best Foods® Light Mayonnaise
- ¼ cup finely chopped drained sun-dried tomatoes packed in oil
- 1 tablespoon grated Parmesan cheese
- 1 loaf Italian or French bread (about 15 inches long), cut into ½-inch slices and toasted

Combine all ingredients except bread in small bowl. Evenly spread artichoke mixture on toasted bread. Broil 1 minute or until golden. Serve immediately.

Spicy Citrus Slaw

MAKES 4 CUPS SLAW

PREP TIME: 15 MINUTES

- 1 cup Hellmann's® or Best Foods® Canola Cholesterol Free Mayonnaise
- 1 can (11 ounces) mandarin oranges, drained (reserve 2 tablespoons syrup)
- 1 tablespoon chopped fresh cilantro (optional)
- 2 teaspoons apple cider vinegar
- ½ teaspoon salt
  Cayenne pepper sauce to taste
- 1 bag (16 ounces) coleslaw mix

Combine Hellmann's® or Best Foods® Canola Cholesterol Free Mayonnaise, reserved syrup, cilantro, vinegar, salt and cayenne pepper sauce in large bowl. Stir in coleslaw mix and oranges. Chill, if desired.

Easy Cheesy Artichoke & Spinach Bread

MAKES 8 SERVINGS

PREP TIME: 10 MINUTES
COOK TIME: 12 MINUTES

- 1 can (14 ounces) artichoke hearts, drained and chopped
- 1 package (10 ounces) frozen chopped spinach or chopped broccoli, thawed and squeezed dry
- 1 cup Hellmann's® or Best Foods® Real Mayonnaise
- 1 cup grated Parmesan cheese
- 1 clove garlic, finely chopped
- 1 loaf French or Italian bread (about 16 inches long), halved lengthwise

1. Preheat oven to 350°F.

2. Combine all ingredients except bread in small bowl; evenly spread on bread. Bake 12 minutes or until golden and heated through.

Creamy Red Potato Salad

MAKES 10 SERVINGS

PREP TIME: 15 MINUTES
COOK TIME: 10 MINUTES

- 3 **pounds red bliss or new potatoes, cut into ¾-inch chunks**
- ¾ **cup Hellmann's® or Best Foods® Real Mayonnaise**
- ½ **cup Wish-Bone® Italian Dressing**
- ½ **cup sliced green onions**
- 1 **teaspoon Dijon mustard**
- 1 **teaspoon lemon juice**
- ⅛ **teaspoon ground black pepper**

1. Cover potatoes with water in 4-quart saucepot; bring to a boil over medium-high heat. Reduce heat to low and simmer, uncovered, 10 minutes or until potatoes are tender. Drain and cool slightly.

2. Combine all ingredients except potatoes in large salad bowl. Add potatoes and toss gently. Serve chilled or at room temperature.

Substitution: Also terrific with Wish-Bone® Robusto Italian or House Italian Dressing.

Southern Spicy Grilled Corn

MAKES 4 SERVINGS

PREP TIME: 8 MINUTES
COOK TIME: 8 MINUTES

- ½ cup Hellmann's® or Best Foods® Real Mayonnaise
- 2 tablespoons chopped onion
- 1 tablespoon apple cider vinegar
- ½ tablespoon finely chopped garlic
- ½ teaspoon ground chipotle chile pepper
- 4 ears corn-on-the-cob, halved

1. Combine all ingredients except corn in small bowl.

2. Grill corn, brushing frequently with Mayonnaise mixture, until corn is tender. Garnish, if desired, with chopped fresh cilantro or parsley.

The Original Potato Salad

MAKES ABOUT 8 SERVINGS

PREP TIME: 10 MINUTES
COOK TIME: 15 MINUTES

It's made with Real Mayonnaise, just like mom always made!

- 2 **pounds potatoes (5 to 6 medium), peeled and cut into ¾-inch chunks**
- 1 **cup Hellmann's® or Best Foods® Real Mayonnaise**
- 2 **tablespoons vinegar**
- 1½ **teaspoons salt**
- 1 **teaspoon sugar**
- ¼ **teaspoon black pepper**
- 1 **cup thinly sliced celery**
- ½ **cup chopped onion**
- 2 **hard-cooked eggs, chopped (optional)**

1. Cover potatoes with water in 4-quart saucepot; bring to a boil over medium-high heat. Reduce heat and simmer 10 minutes or until potatoes are tender. Drain and cool slightly.

2. Combine Hellmann's® or Best Foods® Real Mayonnaise, vinegar, salt, sugar and pepper in large bowl. Add potatoes, celery, onion and eggs and toss gently. Serve chilled or at room temperature.

Substitution: Also terrific with Hellmann's® or Best Foods® Light Mayonnaise or Hellmann's® or Best Foods® Mayonnaise Dressing with Olive Oil.

Black Bean & Corn Salsa

MAKES 4 SERVINGS

PREP TIME: 10 MINUTES

¼ cup Hellmann's® or Best Foods® Real Mayonnaise

2 tablespoons lime juice

½ teaspoon ground cumin

1 can (15 to 19 ounces) black beans, rinsed and drained

1 can (11 ounces) whole kernel corn, drained

1 cup quartered grape tomatoes or cherry tomatoes

½ cup chopped red onion

2 tablespoons chopped fresh cilantro

1 teaspoon chopped jalapeño pepper (optional)

1. Blend Hellmann's® or Best Foods® Real Mayonnaise with lime juice and cumin in medium bowl. Stir in remaining ingredients.

2. Serve chilled or at room temperature.

Serving Suggestion: Serve as a dip with chips or as a side dish with chicken or pork.

Substitution:
Also terrific with Hellmann's® or Best Foods® Canola Cholesterol Free Mayonnaise or Hellmann's® or Best Foods® Light Mayonnaise.

Classic Coleslaw

MAKES 6 CUPS SLAW

PREP TIME: 10 MINUTES

A creamy picnic tradition that cannot be beat with Real Mayonnaise!

- 1 **cup Hellmann's® or Best Foods® Real Mayonnaise**
- 3 **tablespoons lemon juice**
- 2 **tablespoons sugar**
- 1 **teaspoon salt**
- 6 **cups shredded cabbage**
- 1 **cup shredded carrots**
- ½ **cup chopped green bell pepper**

Combine Hellmann's® or Best Foods® Real Mayonnaise, lemon juice, sugar and salt in large bowl. Stir in cabbage, carrots and bell pepper. Chill, if desired.

Substitution: Also terrific with Hellmann's® or Best Foods® Light Mayonnaise or Hellmann's® or Best Foods® Mayonnaise Dressing with Olive Oil.

Disappearing
Buffalo Chicken Dip

MAKES 3 CUPS DIP

PREP TIME: 15 MINUTES
COOK TIME: 20 MINUTES

A dip that truly lives up to its name.

- 2 **cups diced or shredded cooked chicken**
- ⅓ **cup cayenne pepper sauce**
- 1 **cup Hellmann's® or Best Foods® Real or Light Mayonnaise**
- 1 **cup shredded Cheddar cheese (about 4 ounces)**
- 2 **tablespoons finely chopped green onion (optional)**
- 1 **teaspoon lemon juice**
- ¼ **cup crumbled blue cheese**

1. Preheat oven to 375°F.

2. Toss chicken with cayenne pepper sauce. Stir in remaining ingredients except blue cheese. Turn into 1½-quart shallow casserole, then sprinkle with blue cheese.

3. Bake uncovered 20 minutes or until bubbling. Serve, if desired, with celery and/or your favorite dippers.

Farmers Market Veggie Wrapwiches

MAKES 4 SERVINGS

PREP TIME: 10 MINUTES

¼ cup Hellmann's® or Best Foods® Light Mayonnaise

4 (6-inch) fajita-size flour tortillas or garden vegetable wraps

4 slices American, Swiss or Muenster cheese, halved

1 small tomato, cut into 8 wedges

4 cups cut-up vegetables, such as asparagus, red onion, cucumber, bell peppers, alfalfa sprouts and/or shredded carrots

Wish-Bone® Balsamic Vinaigrette Dressing

Spread Hellmann's® or Best Foods® Light Mayonnaise generously onto tortillas. Layer cheese down center of each tortilla. Top with tomato and vegetables, then drizzle with Wish-Bone® Balsamic Vinaigrette Dressing. Roll and fold filled tortilla.

Substitution: Also terrific with Hellmann's® or Best Foods® Real Mayonnaise.

Apple 'n Cheddar Tuna Pitas

MAKES 4 SERVINGS

PREP TIME: 15 MINUTES

- 2 cans (5 ounces each) tuna in water, drained and flaked
- ⅓ cup Hellmann's® or Best Foods® Real Mayonnaise
- ¼ cup finely chopped celery
- ¼ cup diced apple
- ¼ cup dried cranberries
- ¼ cup coarsely chopped walnuts (optional)
- 4 slices Cheddar or American Cheese, cut up
- 2 tablespoons finely chopped red onion (optional)
- 2 (8-inch) plain or whole wheat pita breads, halved

Combine all ingredients except pita breads in medium bowl. Evenly stuff pita breads with tuna mixture.

Substitution: Also terrific with Hellmann's® or Best Foods® Light Mayonnaise or Hellmann's® or Best Foods® Mayonnaise Dressing with Olive Oil.

Creamy Cheddar BLT Turkey Wraps

MAKES 4 SERVINGS

PREP TIME: 15 MINUTES
COOK TIME: 20 SECONDS

- ½ cup shredded Cheddar cheese (about 2 ounces)
- ¼ cup Hellmann's® or Best Foods® Real Mayonnaise
- 2 tablespoons sour cream
- 2 cups cubed cooked turkey or chicken
- 1 small tomato, chopped
- 4 small romaine lettuce leaves
- 4 (10-inch) burrito-size whole wheat or flour tortillas, warmed
- 4 slices cooked bacon

1. Microwave cheese, Hellmann's® or Best Foods® Real Mayonnaise and sour cream in microwave-safe bowl at HIGH 20 seconds; stir until smooth. Stir in turkey and tomato.

2. Arrange lettuce on centers of each tortilla, then top with turkey mixture and bacon.

3. Roll up and secure with toothpicks. Slice in half diagonally and serve.

Tuna & Bow Tie Salad

MAKES 4 SERVINGS

PREP TIME: 15 MINUTES
COOK TIME: 20 MINUTES

- 8 ounces whole grain or regular bow tie pasta
- 6 tablespoons Hellmann's® or Best Foods® Light Mayonnaise
- 2 tablespoons red wine vinegar
- 2 tablespoons chopped fresh basil leaves OR 1 teaspoon dried basil, crushed
- 1 clove garlic, finely chopped
- ¼ teaspoon ground black pepper
- 2 cups cherry tomatoes, quartered OR grape tomatoes, halved
- 2 cans (5 ounces each) tuna, drained and flaked
- 1 package (9 ounces) frozen green beans, thawed
- ⅓ cup chopped red onion

1. Cook bow ties according to package directions; drain and rinse with cold water until completely cool.

2. Combine Hellmann's® or Best Foods® Light Mayonnaise, vinegar, basil, garlic and pepper in large bowl.

3. Add remaining ingredients; toss well. Chill, if desired.

Substitution: Also terrific with Hellmann's® or Best Foods® Mayonnaise Dressing with Olive Oil.

Hellmann's® Easiest-Ever Sandwich Spreads

MAKES ½ TO ¾ CUP SPREAD

PREP TIME: 5 MINUTES

**By simply adding just two or three ingredients
to Hellmann's® Mayonnaise
you can make these delicious sandwich spreads!**

**½ cup Hellmann's® or Best Foods® Real or Light
Mayonnaise**

Stir the following ingredients into ½ cup Hellmann's® or Best Foods® Real or Light Mayonnaise:

For a **CREAMY CAESAR SPREAD,** stir in ¼ cup grated Parmesan cheese, 1 tablespoon lemon juice and 1 teaspoon garlic powder.

For a **GARLIC 'N ROASTED RED PEPPER SPREAD,** stir in 1 jar (7 ounces) roasted red peppers, drained and finely chopped, ½ teaspoon red wine vinegar and 1 clove finely chopped garlic.

For a **WASABI SPREAD,** stir in 3 tablespoons prepared wasabi and 1 tablespoon EACH lime juice and chopped cilantro.

For a **BLUE CHEESE 'N BACON SPREAD,** stir in ¼ cup crumbled blue cheese and 2 slices crisp-cooked crumbled bacon.

For a **BUFFALO SPREAD,** stir in 1 tablespoon cayenne pepper sauce and 1 tablespoon chopped parsley.

For a **FRESH ITALIAN HERB SPREAD,** stir in 1 tablespoon EACH chopped basil and oregano, 1 clove finely chopped garlic and 1 tablespoon red wine vinegar.

For a **SMOKEY CHIPOTLE SPREAD,** stir in 1 clove finely chopped garlic, 1 tablespoon lime juice and ½ teaspoon chipotle pepper.

Hearty Roast Beef Sandwich with Provolone

MAKES 1 SERVING

PREP TIME: 10 MINUTES

- 1 tablespoon Hellmann's® or Best Foods® Light Mayonnaise
- ⅛ teaspoon garlic powder
- 2 slices whole grain bread
- 1 leaf green or red leaf lettuce
- 2 slices tomato
- 1 ounce sliced provolone cheese
- 3 ounces thinly sliced deli roast beef

Combine Hellmann's® or Best Foods® Light Mayonnaise with garlic powder in small bowl; spread on 1 bread slice. Top with lettuce, tomato, cheese and roast beef, then remaining bread slice.

Variation: For a great twist, try using ⅛ teaspoon dry wasabi powder instead of garlic powder.

Chicken Niçoise Salad

MAKES 6 SERVINGS

PREP TIME: 30 MINUTES
COOK TIME: 12 MINUTES

- ⅓ **cup Hellmann's® or Best Foods® Mayonnaise Dressing with Olive Oil**
- ⅓ **cup Wish-Bone® Italian Dressing**
- 1 **pound boneless, skinless chicken breast halves**
- 8 **cups mixed salad greens**
- 8 **ounces green beans, halved, blanched and cooled**
- 8 **ounces new potatoes, quartered, cooked and cooled**
- ¼ **small red onion, thinly sliced**
- ¼ **cup sliced niçoise or oil-cured olives**
- 1 **cup cherry tomatoes, halved**
- 2 **hard-cooked eggs, sliced**

1. Combine Hellmann's® or Best Foods® Mayonnaise Dressing with Olive Oil with Wish-Bone® Italian Dressing in small bowl. Reserve 2 tablespoons; set aside.

2. Grill or broil chicken, turning once and brushing with reserved Mayonnaise mixture, 12 minutes or until chicken is thoroughly cooked. Cool, then cut into cubes.

3. Arrange greens on large serving platter, then top with chicken, green beans, potatoes, onion, olives, tomatoes and eggs. Just before serving, toss with Mayonnaise mixture.

Light Meals — 28

California Chicken Wraps

MAKES 4 SERVINGS

PREP TIME: 10 MINUTES

- 3 tablespoons Hellmann's® or Best Foods® Mayonnaise Dressing with Olive Oil
- 4 (6-inch) fajita size whole wheat flour tortillas
- 12 ounces boneless, skinless chicken breast halves, grilled and sliced
- 1 medium avocado, peeled and sliced
- 1 red bell pepper, sliced
- ¼ cup sliced red onion
- 2 cups mixed salad greens

1. Spread It: Spread tortillas with Hellmann's® or Best Foods® Mayonnaise Dressing with Olive Oil.

2. Stuff It: Layer chicken, avocado, red pepper, red onion and salad greens down center of each tortilla.

3. Wrap It: Roll and fold the filled tortilla.

Substitution: Also terrific with Hellmann's® or Best Foods® Real Mayonnaise or Hellmann's® or Best Foods® Light Mayonnaise.

Pasta Salad with Grilled Vegetables

MAKES 8 SERVINGS

PREP TIME: 20 MINUTES
COOK TIME: 25 MINUTES

- 1 **cup Hellmann's® or Best Foods® Mayonnaise Dressing with Olive Oil, divided**
- 2 **tablespoons balsamic vinegar**
- ½ **teaspoon black pepper**
- 6 **cups assorted fresh vegetables (zucchini, red and yellow bell peppers and/or red onion), sliced**
- 1 **box (16 ounces) fusilli pasta, cooked, drained and cooled**
- 1 **cup loosely packed fresh basil leaves, chopped**
- ⅓ **cup sliced kalamata or pitted ripe olives**

1. Blend ¼ cup Hellmann's® or Best Foods® Mayonnaise Dressing with Olive Oil, vinegar and black pepper in medium bowl. Stir in vegetables. Arrange vegetable mixture in grill pan or on foil on grill. Grill vegetables, stirring once, 20 minutes or until vegetables are crisp-tender. Cool.

2. Combine vegetables with remaining ingredients in large bowl. Serve immediately or cover and refrigerate until ready to serve.

Tip: Add cut up cooked chicken or flaked drained tuna for a simple main dish idea.

Note: Vegetables may also be roasted in the oven.

Mediterranean Turkey Sandwiches

MAKES 2 SERVINGS

PREP TIME: 10 MINUTES

- ½ cup **Hellmann's® or Best Foods® Light Mayonnaise**
- 1 teaspoon **balsamic vinegar**
- ½ teaspoon **dried Italian seasoning, crushed**
- 4 slices **artisan or whole grain bread, grilled or lightly toasted**
- 2 **green leaf lettuce leaves**
- 2 slices **Swiss cheese (about 2 ounces)**
- 4 slices **tomato**
- 4 slices **cooked turkey (about 6 ounces)**
- **Sliced red onion (optional)**

Combine Hellmann's® or Best Foods® Light Mayonnaise, vinegar and Italian seasoning in small bowl. Spread each slice of bread with Mayonnaise mixture. Evenly top 2 slices of bread with lettuce, cheese, tomato, turkey and onion, then top with remaining 2 bread slices. Garnish, if desired, with pickles.

Substitution: Also terrific with Hellmann's® or Best Foods® Real Mayonnaise or Hellmann's® or Best Foods® Canola Cholesterol Free Mayonnaise.

Italian Combo Sandwich

MAKES 1 SERVING

PREP TIME: 10 MINUTES

The simple addition of a few ingredients
turns a ho-hum sandwich into an amazing one.

- **1 tablespoon Hellmann's® or Best Foods® Light Mayonnaise**
- **2 slices multigrain bread**
- **2 tablespoons chopped marinated artichokes (optional)**
- **2 tablespoons sliced hot Italian peppers (optional)**
- **2 ounces thinly sliced deli ham**
- **1 slice mozzarella or provolone cheese**
- **¼ cup baby arugula or spinach leaves**

Evenly spread Hellmann's® or Best Foods® Light Mayonnaise
on 1 bread slice, then top with artichokes and Italian
peppers. Layer with remaining ingredients, then top with
remaining bread.

Chipotle Roast Beef Sandwich with Pepper Jack

MAKES 1 SERVING

PREP TIME: 10 MINUTES

- 1 **tablespoon Hellmann's® or Best Foods® Light Mayonnaise**
- ¼ **teaspoon ground chipotle chile pepper**
- 1 **seeded Kaiser roll, split**
- 3 **ounces thinly sliced deli roast beef**
- 1 **ounces sliced pepper Jack cheese**
- ¼ **cup watercress or lettuce**

Combine Hellmann's® or Best Foods® Light Mayonnaise with chipotle chile pepper in small bowl; spread on bottom half of roll. Top with roast beef, cheese and watercress, then top half of roll.

Variation: For another tasty topping that's perfect for roast beef, grilled burgers, steak or any sandwich, add horseradish to Hellmann's® or Best Foods® Real Mayonnaise.

Parmesan Crusted Chicken

MAKES 4 SERVINGS

PREP TIME: 10 MINUTES
COOK TIME: 20 MINUTES

**Hellmann's® transforms your chicken
into a juicier, crispier, more delicious meal.**

- ½ **cup Hellmann's® or Best Foods® Light Mayonnaise**
- ¼ **cup grated Parmesan cheese**
- 4 **boneless, skinless chicken breast halves (about 1¼ pounds)**
- 4 **teaspoons Italian seasoned dry bread crumbs**

1. Preheat oven to 425°F.

2. Combine Hellmann's® or Best Foods® Light Mayonnaise with cheese in medium bowl. Arrange chicken on baking sheet. Evenly top with Mayonnaise mixture, then sprinkle with bread crumbs.

3. Bake 20 minutes or until chicken is thoroughly cooked.

Substitution: Also terrific with Hellmann's® or Best Foods® Light Mayonnaise or Hellmann's® or Best Foods® Canola Cholesterol Free Mayonnaise.

Turkey Burgers with Pesto-Red Pepper Mayonnaise

MAKES 4 SERVINGS

PREP TIME: 10 MINUTES
COOK TIME: 8 MINUTES

¼ cup Hellmann's® or Best Foods® Light
    Mayonnaise

1 tablespoon prepared pesto

1 tablespoon finely chopped roasted red pepper

4 turkey burgers

4 Kaiser or whole grain rolls

  Tomato slices

  Lettuce leaves

  Onion slices (optional)

1. Combine Hellmann's® or Best Foods® Light Mayonnaise, pesto and roasted pepper in small bowl; set aside.

2. Grill or broil turkey burgers 8 minutes or until thoroughly cooked, turning once. To serve, evenly spread Mayonnaise mixture on rolls, then top with burgers, tomato, lettuce, onion and dollop of remaining Mayonnaise mixture.

Variation: To perk up the flavor of your burgers, mix Wish-Bone® Italian Dressing into the ground turkey.

Substitution: Also terrific with Hellmann's® or Best Foods® Low Fat Mayonnaise Dressing or Hellmann's® or Best Foods® Canola Cholesterol Free Mayonnaise.

Quesadilla Burgers

MAKES 4 SERVINGS

PREP TIME: 20 MINUTES
COOK TIME: 12 MINUTES

¼ cup Hellmann's® or Best Foods® Real
  Mayonnaise

¼ teaspoon ground chipotle chile pepper

1 medium tomato, chopped

1 avocado, peeled and chopped

¼ cup chopped red onion

1 cup shredded Cheddar cheese (about 4 ounces)

4 (8-inch) soft taco-size whole wheat or flour
  tortillas

4 hamburger patties, cooked and halved

1. Combine Hellmann's® or Best Foods® Real Mayonnaise with chipotle chile pepper in medium bowl. Stir in tomato, avocado and red onion; set aside.

2. Evenly sprinkle ½ of the cheese on 1 side of each tortilla, then top each with 2 burger halves, tomato mixture and remaining cheese; fold over. Cook quesadillas, 2 at a time, in 12-inch nonstick skillet over medium heat, carefully turning once, 6 minutes or until cheese is melted and tortillas are golden. Repeat with remaining quesadillas.

Substitution: Try using turkey, chicken or veggie patties!

Smoked Ham, Swiss & Caramelized Onion Sandwich

MAKES 1 SERVING

PREP TIME: 10 MINUTES

- 1 tablespoon Hellmann's® or Best Foods® Real Mayonnaise
- 1 multigrain Kaiser roll
- 2 thin slices deli smoked ham (about 2 ounces)
- 2 thin slices Swiss cheese (about 2 ounces)
  Caramelized onions (recipe follows)
- 2 slices tomato (optional)
- 1 green leaf lettuce leaf

Evenly spread Hellmann's® or Best Foods® Real Mayonnaise on roll, then top with remaining ingredients.

Note: It takes a little time to caramelize the onion, but it's well worth it.

Caramelized Onions: Melt 2 tablespoons Country Crock® Spread in 10-inch nonstick skillet over medium-high heat and cook 1 thinly sliced medium onion, stirring occasionally, until dark golden brown and very tender, about 10 minutes.

Pork Chops with Creamy Lime Salsa

MAKES 4 SERVINGS

PREP TIME: 10 MINUTES
COOK TIME: 15 MINUTES

- ½ cup Hellmann's® or Best Foods® Light Mayonnaise
- 1 tablespoon lime juice
- ¼ cup finely chopped red onion
- 1 clove garlic, finely chopped
- ¼ teaspoon grated lime peel (optional)
- ⅛ teaspoon black pepper
- 4 large boneless pork chops, ¾ inch thick* (about 1 pound)
- 1 tablespoon Jamaican jerk seasoning
- 1 medium mango, seeded, peeled and cut into 8 slices (optional)

Try substituting boneless, skinless chicken breast halves or halibut steaks for pork chops.

1. For Creamy Lime Salsa, combine Hellmann's® or Best Foods® Light Mayonnaise, lime juice, onion, garlic, lime peel and pepper in medium bowl; set aside.

2. Evenly season chops with jerk seasoning. Grill or broil chops until done. Arrange chops on serving platter, then evenly garnish with mango and Creamy Lime Salsa. Serve with remaining salsa.

Note: Jamaican jerk seasoning usually features allspice, Scotch bonnet peppers and thyme.

Substitution: Also terrific with Hellmann's® or Best Foods® Low Fat Mayonnaise Dressing or Hellmann's® or Best Foods® Canola Cholesterol Free Mayonnaise.

Parmesan-Crusted Eggplant Sandwiches

MAKES 4 SERVINGS

PREP TIME: 20 MINUTES
COOK TIME: 15 MINUTES

Enjoy these hearty sandwiches for lunch or dinner.
Great for on-the-go.

- 1 **medium eggplant, cut into ½-inch-thick rounds**
- ½ **cup Hellmann's® or Best Foods® Real Mayonnaise**
- ¼ **cup grated Parmesan cheese**
- 1 **clove garlic, chopped**
- 4 **teaspoons Italian seasoned dry bread crumbs**
- 8 **ounces fresh mozzarella cheese, thinly sliced**
- 4 **hoagie or Italian rolls, split and toasted**
- 2 **medium tomatoes, thinly sliced**

1. Preheat oven to 425°F. Line baking sheet, if desired, with aluminum foil sprayed with no-stick cooking spray. Arrange eggplant on baking sheet; set aside.

2. Combine Hellmann's® or Best Foods® Real Mayonnaise, Parmesan cheese and garlic in small bowl. Evenly spread eggplant with Mayonnaise mixture, then sprinkle with bread crumbs. Bake 15 minutes or until eggplant is golden and tender.

3. Arrange mozzarella on rolls, then top with tomatoes and eggplant.

Parmesan-Crusted Bruschetta Chicken

MAKES 4 SERVINGS

PREP TIME: 15 MINUTES
COOK TIME: 20 MINUTES

The fresh flavors of Bruschetta top perfectly moist chicken.

- ⅓ **cup Hellmann's® or Best Foods® Mayonnaise Dressing with Olive Oil**
- 3 **tablespoons grated Parmesan cheese**
- 4 **boneless, skinless chicken breast halves (about 1¼ pounds)**
- 4 **teaspoons plain dry bread crumbs**
- 1 **tablespoon Italian seasoning**
- 2 **medium tomatoes, seeded and chopped**
- ¼ **cup chopped red onion**
- ¼ **cup Wish-Bone® Robusto Italian Dressing or Wish-Bone® Italian Dressing**

1. Preheat oven to 425°F.

2. Combine Hellmann's® or Best Foods® Mayonnaise Dressing with Olive Oil with cheese in medium bowl. Arrange chicken on baking sheet. Evenly top with Mayonnaise mixture, then sprinkle with bread crumbs and Italian seasoning.

3. Bake 20 minutes or until chicken is thoroughly cooked.

4. Meanwhile, combine remaining ingredients in medium bowl.

5. To serve, evenly top chicken with bruschetta mixture.

Substitution: Also terrific with Hellmann's® or Best Foods® Real Mayonnaise or Hellmann's® or Best Foods® Light Mayonnaise.

Creamy Loaded Mashed Potatoes

MAKES 8 SERVINGS

PREP TIME: 10 MINUTES
COOK TIME: 45 MINUTES

- 3 **pounds all-purpose potatoes, peeled and cubed**
- 1½ **cups shredded Cheddar cheese (about 6 ounces), divided**
- 1 **cup Hellmann's® or Best Foods® Real Mayonnaise**
- 1 **cup sour cream**
- 3 **green onions, finely chopped**
- 6 **slices bacon or turkey bacon, crisp-cooked and crumbled, divided (optional)**

1. Preheat oven to 375°F. Spray 2-quart shallow baking dish with no-stick cooking spray; set aside.

2. Cover potatoes with water in 4-quart saucepot; bring to a boil over high heat. Reduce heat to low and cook 10 minutes or until potatoes are tender; drain and mash.

3. Stir in 1 cup cheese, Hellmann's® or Best Foods® Real Mayonnaise, sour cream, green onions and 4 strips crumbled bacon. Turn into prepared baking dish and bake 30 minutes or until bubbling.

4. Top with remaining ½ cup cheese and bacon. Bake an additional 5 minutes or until cheese is melted. Garnish, if desired, with additional chopped green onions.

Tuscan Glazed Chicken

MAKES 6 SERVINGS

PREP TIME: 10 MINUTES
COOK TIME: 20 MINUTES

- ⅓ cup Hellmann's® or Best Foods® Mayonnaise Dressing with Olive Oil
- 3 tablespoons finely chopped roasted red pepper
- 1 teaspoon garlic powder
- 1 teaspoon balsamic vinegar
- ½ teaspoon Italian seasoning
- 6 boneless, skinless chicken breast halves (about 2 pounds)

1. Preheat oven to 425°F.

2. Combine all ingredients except chicken in medium bowl. Arrange chicken on baking sheet, then evenly top with Mayonnaise mixture.

3. Bake 20 minutes or until chicken is thoroughly cooked.

Grilled Ham 'n Cheese

MAKES 2 SERVINGS

PREP TIME: 5 MINUTES
COOK TIME: 5 MINUTES

- 4 **slices your favorite bread**
- 4 **slices boiled or honey baked deli ham**
- 4 **slices American, Cheddar or your favorite cheese**
- 2 **large slices tomato**
- 2 **tablespoons Hellmann's® or Best Foods® Real Mayonnaise**

1. Assemble sandwiches with bread, ham, cheese and tomato. Spread outside of sandwiches with Hellmann's® or Best Foods® Real Mayonnaise.

2. Cook sandwiches in 12-inch skillet over medium heat, turning once, 5 minutes or until golden brown and cheese is melted.

Substitution: Also terrific with deli turkey and Hellmann's® or Best Foods® Light Mayonnaise.

Easy Warm Dinner Sandwich

MAKES 6 SERVINGS

PREP TIME: 10 MINUTES
COOK TIME: 25 MINUTES

Many families enjoy sandwiches for dinner. They're easy to make and great on-the-go.

- 1 loaf unsliced round bread (about 9 inches in diameter)
- ¼ cup Hellmann's® or Best Foods® Real Mayonnaise
- 8 ounces sliced deli ham and/or turkey breast
- 4 ounces sliced American cheese
- 1 large tomato, sliced
- 2 tablespoons Wish-Bone® Balsamic Italian Vinaigrette Dressing

1. Preheat oven to 350°F.

2. Cut bread in half horizontally; hollow out center of each half, leaving ¼-inch shell. Spread Hellmann's® or Best Foods® Real Mayonnaise onto bottom half. Layer ham, cheese and tomato. Drizzle with Wish-Bone® Balsamic Italian Vinaigrette Dressing; replace top shell.

3. Wrap in aluminum foil and bake 25 minutes or until heated through. To serve, cut into wedges.

Super-Moist Cornbread

MAKES 8 SERVINGS

PREP TIME: 5 MINUTES
COOK TIME: 25 MINUTES

- **1 can (11 ounces) Mexican-style corn, drained**
- **1 package (8½ ounces) corn muffin mix**
- **½ cup Hellmann's® or Best Foods® Real Mayonnaise**
- **1 egg, slightly beaten**

1. Preheat oven to 400°F. Spray 8-inch round cake pan with no-stick cooking spray; set aside.

2. Combine all ingredients in medium bowl until moistened. Evenly spread in prepared pan.

3. Bake 25 minutes or until toothpick inserted into center comes out clean.

Toasted Tuna 'n Bacon Melts

MAKES 4 SERVINGS

PREP TIME: 15 MINUTES
COOK TIME: 5 MINUTES

This is really easy to make in your toaster oven.

- 2 cans (5 ounces each) tuna, drained and flaked
- ½ cup finely chopped celery
- ½ cup Hellmann's® or Best Foods® Real Mayonnaise
- 4 slices your favorite bread, toasted
- 4 slices American, Swiss or Cheddar cheese
- 4 slices bacon or turkey bacon, halved and cooked

1. Preheat oven to 400°F.

2. Combine tuna, celery and Hellmann's® or Best Foods® Real Mayonnaise in medium bowl. Evenly spread tuna mixture on bread slices, then top with cheese and bacon.

3. Arrange bread on cookie sheet and bake 5 minutes or until cheese is melted.